RICH SLOW

Is My Homeboy

Real Estate Investing Redefined

Debbie Trominski

Produced by BookCreate
Seattle, Washington USA

Printed in USA

ISBN 978-0-578-61251-5

DebbieTrominski.com

Cover illustration by Vivian Trominski

The author is a licensed real estate broker in the State of Texas.
This book is for informational purposes only and is not intended to
give legal, accounting, tax, financial, or investment advice. Readers
are encouraged to seek the advice of professionals in each of these
domains. The author specifically disclaims any liability, loss, or risk
which is incurred as a consequence, directly or indirectly, of the use
and application of any of the contents of this book.

DEDICATION

This book is for Carl, Vivian and Hazel whom I love best of all. It's for my brother, Jeff, who has encouraged my investment efforts for years and, more recently, my book-writing efforts. It's also dedicated to my parents who make me drive them to see my houses when they come visit.

ACKNOWLEDGMENTS

I'd like to thank the people in my life who have inspired and traveled the investment journey with me. First there is Charles who got me started and has guided me for years in investing. Then there are my agent buddies, Tanya and Cindy, who have compared notes with me as we've navigated this together. Finally, to my clients who have put their trust in me to lead them on the investment path with a special shout out to Ernesto and Olga who are some of my most enthusiastic supporters. You guys, I wrote a book! Isn't this cool?

REVIEWS

Rich Slow Is My Homeboy is an eye opening read that will explain in simple and fun terms a solid long-term investment methodology. Most people find investing a daunting only-for-the-rich proposition. This is easy read reveals how it is attainable and within reach for most, walking the reader through the steps to ensure success. It is not a recipe to become rich overnight, but a roadmap for becoming wealthy and financially independent.

~ *Ernesto Del Valle Lehne*

I loved this book! As an armchair investor who has always sat on the sidelines and watched other people invest while I worried about the staying on top of multiple mortgages, this book gave me a clear and informative map of how to invest in property. Debbie's voice and humor jumps out from each page and mixes practical definitions of different strategies with stories from her own personal journey in property investment and management. Based on the content, I finally got a hold on the differences between Home Equity Loans, Home Equity Lines of Credit, and cash-out refinances, and I appreciated her laddering approach to slowly building up equity that can support a comfortable retirement. I'm ready to start with purchasing the first of my very own "little green Monopoly houses."

~ *Sally P.*

This is a great book that shows a path towards a great retirement by taking advantage of rental home ownership. It does a complete job of providing everything you need to know to pursue this unique investment strategy. Debbie's personal experience given in the book is proof of the kind of success this strategy can have.

~ Jeremy G.

LOVE the irreverent, playful tone throughout - "if mortgages can be called sexy, this one was x-rated"! LOL. There is a plethora of data & charts -> this really underscores the credibility of the methodology and, if anything, the numbers speak for themselves. Overall, the book is a "snackable" length and full of interesting concepts and compelling data. Bravo!

~ Anna S.

TABLE OF CONTENTS

CHAPTER 1   A Happy Ending   2

CHAPTER 2   Getting Rich Slow   7

CHAPTER 3   Uncle Sam Wants You to Invest   14

CHAPTER 4   Honey, You Need Money   16

CHAPTER 5   Pick a Winner   21

CHAPTER 6   Climbing the Retirement Ladder   29

CHAPTER 7   Yeah But   35

CHAPTER 8   Nerdy Stuff You Might be Wondering About   39

CHAPTER 9   Final Words   44

INTRODUCTION

This is a book inspired by my friends and clients who eagerly engage me in conversations about real estate investing. This book is meant for those of you who are ready to start the process of getting your first investment property, or at least have some curiosity about investing. I imagine my experience and advice will resonate with individuals and couples somewhere in the middle-class spectrum as far as the income they produce. It's not for everyone, but if you can afford your own home, you can start to build your own portfolio one step at a time. I'm neither a financial advisor, mortgage professional, CPA, qualified intermediary nor attorney. I am a licensed real estate broker in Texas with an exciting story to share of how I have turned one house into eleven houses—a story that is repeatable and duplicable—while focusing on my day job and raising a family.

Real estate is a powerful, timeless path to building wealth. It's been such a good investment vehicle for so long that I think it might be the world's second oldest way to make money. If you are able to purchase property in the US, you have relatively unfettered access to get into this game as compared to our ancestors from centuries past as well as our modern counterparts in other countries. We are fortunate indeed.

CHAPTER ONE

A Happy Ending

How'd you like to retire in style with paying little to no taxes? The unsettling truth is that just saving through traditional 401(k) or IRA methods might not get you there. As the Baby Boomers are finding out, you've got to be faster, smarter and more intentional about investing if you want to live a good life for the projected 25+ years of old age that statistics say most of us will live after retirement age. Living in retirement without enough money to get you to the grave (or urn) means living in a state of constant compromise and stress that can cut your life short. Gross!

And if you think you'll be employable at a high level of income much past the age of sixty, look again. How many 65- to 70-year-olds have highly compensated roles at your place of employment? How many 65- to 70-year-olds are at your company at all? And do you really want to be working when you're that age? Maybe you'd rather be traveling, chilling with grandbabies and trying out new hobbies. Or you could be content to stay at home and watch *Wheel of Fortune* and *Jeopardy*. Either way, ain't nobody really wants to hold down a job once you turn gray.

This paragraph has lots of numbers. Just take it slow and refer to the exhibit on the next page as another way of looking at the numbers. Let's say in today's dollars it takes a minimum annual income of

$200k to live a good life in old age without suffering. Living without suffering financially looks like dining out at nice restaurants, traveling well, pursuing hobbies, spoiling grandbabies, leaving a financial legacy for your family or other worthy causes, living in housing you like, and getting good medical help. It doesn't look like clipping coupons, eating dog food and living with your kids as a last resort before homelessness. If you don't believe me check your numbers very honestly and consult with your financial advisor. That means a couple needs to have $5M in capital at work (net income minus the equity in your home) to enjoy an annual income of $200k without depleting your principal. How's that math work? Using historical data let's assume the stock market will continue to return an average of 7% a year and inflation will continue to average 3% a year. That leaves 4% of your capital at work that you can tap each year without killing the golden goose that is your capital at work: 4% of $5M is $200k. Make sense? I hope so.

Why can't you include the equity in your home? Because you have to

RETIRING IN STYLE
How to pay yourself $200K a year

Capital at work:	$5,000,000
Assumed annual growth rate: 7%	=350,000
MINUS assumed inflation of 3%	−150,000
EQUALS available withdrawal 4%	=200,000

live somewhere, silly! That money is otherwise occupied, providing a roof over your cute little head.

So if you need to get at least $5M accumulated before you retire and you have a spouse or partner, you can just split the duty and each of you bring home at least $2.5M extra while you also work to provide for your family in the present. Oh wait, that might suck and put you in a mood of despair. Don't worry, I've got a plan to share with you that replaces the need for you to save $5M in retirement funds and it doesn't require you to increase your current level of pre-retirement income. Remember how I asked if you'd like to retire in style and with minimal taxes? Keep reading and I'll explain.

While this is another book about investing in real estate, it's not another book to tell you to get creative, cunning, crafty, aggressive, sleazy and otherwise slick and scheming. Nope, this is a fairly basic get rich slow path to wealth that doesn't have you trying to bottom feed or otherwise try conniving ways to "always buy off market at wholesale," "make hundreds of lowball offers," "find alternative forms of financing," "exploit distressed sellers" and other arguably unctuous ways of getting into the game. The very notion that you have to pull together creative ways of investing or know the right people turns a lot of people off before they start. Why make it so hard by chasing a needle in a haystack when there are plenty of good opportunities passing you by every day that are available through straightforward, traditional methods? Most of us don't have time to play the clever game as we are focused on taking care of our families and earning a living. My method is so simple and pure, yet uncommon enough that most people are unaware of their options. If you can afford to own your own home and are a generally normal person, you are already well on your way. Let me explain.

First, this method involves buying and holding single family homes in a market that has strong fundamentals for appreciation. It's not about investing in slowly appreciating markets that have strong monthly cash flow. For those of you who require both cash flow and appreciation, ha! I require an athletic figure while eating like crap. That's not going to happen for either of us. A real estate market is either oriented toward appreciation or cash flow. If there was an amazing place that offered both, the super-rich would have already exploited it and us regular folk wouldn't have access to it.

Now that I have you snapped out of the imaginary world of cash flow and appreciation happening all at once, let me redefine these ideas for you. The way I practice investing is to look at appreciation AS being a form of cash flow. The difference is that the cash flow shows up every four to seven years, depending on how the market is performing, as a lump sum instead of a monthly stream. And my method lets you get this lump sum tax-free without selling the property. How in the world does that work?

Let's take a few moments to explain a concept that is critical to this text, the cash-out refinance. As you will learn by reading this book, this financing vehicle is instrumental in growing an investment portfolio and providing cash in retirement years—tax free! A cash-out refinance is a mortgage loan whereby you refinance your existing mortgage and pull the equity that has been locked up in your home. Say what? Suppose you owe $100,000 on your house but today it's

CASHOUT REFINANCE

Free up capital for your next investment

- A cashout refinance is a new mortgage that is larger than your current mortgage.
- This can happen because your home has appreciated and/or you have paid down your current mortgage.
- The new mortgage is used to pay off the old mortgage and you get paid the difference between the two loan amounts.
- The amount you receive is not taxable.

FOR EXAMPLE:

Current market value:	$200,000
Maximum new loan amount 75%	= 150,000
Existing loan amount	− 100,000
Cash Proceeds	= 50,000

- The maximum new loan amount is based on a 75% LTV of the appraised market value in this example.
- LTV is loan-to-value ratio. Lenders require a minimum of 20-25% equity cushion to remain in the property, you can not get a mortgage for the entire property value, just up to 75-80% of it's value.
- Owner occupied homes can get up to an 80% LTV where a 20% equity cushion remains.
- Investor properties can go has high as a 75% LTV where a 25% equity cushion remains.

RICH SLOW IS MY HOMEBOY

worth $200,000. You can refinance the home where you pull out 75% of the current market value and receive it as cash. That means you can get a mortgage for $150,000 and when the refinance is completed, your previous mortgage is paid off and you get to pocket the $50,000 difference. It's a lot like selling the house to yourself. You get to enjoy the equity now and hold onto the asset. Win-win! It gets better: the $50,000 you received in this example is tax-free because the IRS doesn't consider the money received in the cash-out refinance to be income since this amount must be repaid. This example ignores closing costs, but I want you to get the big picture of how a cash-out refinance works. See the accompanying table for another look at how it comes together.

CHAPTER TWO

Getting Rich Slow

This isn't smack talk. Let me tell you my story so you can see that I'm putting my money where my mouth is. I have a husband and kids that I love very much, so I'm quite serious and as risk-averse as possible. My husband and I bought our first house in 1998 when I was only twenty-four. We put the minimum down on a place in a shaggy neighborhood that was adjacent to the University of Texas at Austin and the Mueller airport and not too far from downtown. I didn't fancy myself a princess and require new construction and gobs of space. I was more interested in being close to bars and clubs back then. That paid off big time! Before long Austin grew and grew and the airport moved to a new location far away from our house and Mueller became an urban Mecca of shopping, parks and densely built housing. Fast forward twenty-plus years and this (still to this day shaggy and very "Austin") neighborhood is hella expensive. Had we bought a starter house in the burbs we would have never gotten anywhere close to where we are now. This house was "patient zero" in our portfolio of eleven homes (and counting). To date we have owned fourteen homes and have built our portfolio based on the original equity of our first home with the exception of one property for which I used out-of-pocket savings to make the down payment.

So, how did this one little bungalow we got for less than $115k turn into a $3M portfolio in twenty-one years? Before I tell you, I should point out that's a compound annual growth rate of 16.8%! We did it by reinvesting the equity through traditional, conventional lending methods. Nothing slick. I don't do slick. I don't have time for that, and I lack the creativity to come up with cold calling and expensive mass mailing schemes to find a "killer deal."

Our first house, which I will now refer to as "Shaggy" appreciated nicely because of its sweet, sweet location. We lived happily in Shaggy and five years after we moved there, I became a real estate agent. Thanks to my broker, I was woke about the power of building wealth through real estate. I figured if I was going to sell real estate for a living, I should put my money where my mouth is all the while making myself a better leader for my clients. By this point we had a good amount of equity built up in Shaggy. By doing a cash-out refinance on the property we pulled out cash, tax-free cash! The cash was used to put down the 20% down payment need for our first rental.

You could say that Shaggy had a baby! She seeded her own house based on her increase in value. We didn't have to tap into savings... back then we probably had next to no savings as I wasn't even thirty yet. I can't remember those details (bars and clubs!). Hey, I should mention not to be put out that I started so early and you might be well past your twenties. This philosophy is solid for anyone into their fifties. You might be in a better spot than I am in many ways because I have been self-employed as a Realtor since 2003 and haven't had the glory of an employer-sponsored 401(k) with matching funds since I left the corporate world in 2000 to get my MBA. But this isn't a case of whose is bigger. It's about getting to a better spot than where you are now. And I really want that for you because of what it can produce for your financial legacy.

Back to Shaggy's baby, our first investment property. It's a moral question of whether the ends justify the means, but in this case I'll go with the notion that they do. I purchased an investment home somewhat impulsively and I consistently lost money on it every month. I'm not opposed to being slightly cash-flow negative, but this was slightly more than slightly negative. The good news is that I chose the right location again and the house appreciated by 40% over the next two years. At that point I sold it and used a 1031 Tax Deferred Exchange to purchase two more rentals. A bit more on 1031 Tax Deferred Exchanges is on the following page.

I bought subsequent rentals through various means. One home I purchased in 2005 when mortgage money was fast and loose

TRADE IN YOUR OLD PROPERTY

Using a 1031 Tax Deferred Exchange

A 1031 Tax Deferred Exchange is a process in which an investor can sell their investment property and reinvest the proceeds into more investment properties in order to defer capital gains taxes and depreciation recapture.

There are specific rules to executing a 1031 Exchange that must be followed exactly.

A Qualified Intermediary is a professional that handles these exchanges and can give you more details on how they work for you and your situation.

It is also prudent to consult with a CPA when considering a 1031 Exchange.

with an interest-only zero down loan. If loans can be sexy this was X-rated! Another one was purchased with the profits when we sold Shaggy to upgrade homes to raise children in. One was purchased with cash on hand because I had a great year selling homes and needed to hide the money from myself by putting it into a home before I did something stupid with it. Not too long after that we used a home equity line of credit (HELOC) on our current primary residence to get another one. HELOCs are explained on the next page.

Fast forward to 2016—we had a portfolio of five rentals, and I had never extracted any equity from any of them. This is when I really discovered the power of the cash-out refinance. We pulled equity out of all five homes and walked away with $300k. This $300k is not considered income by the IRS and was not taxable, so the whole chunk was ours to do with as we pleased. We basically sold the houses to ourselves. We got to access the equity and still hold onto these well-performing assets. Sure, the new mortgages were more expensive than the old ones and our monthly cash flow diminished, but who cares when you have $300k in the bank! This isn't a monthly cash flow play in the traditional sense. Remember when I said that appreciation IS your cash flow. It's just deferred to show up in large chunks every few years or so.

We took this $300k and turned it into five more rentals. These houses all had babies of their own without taking any money out of our savings. One cool thing that my mortgage lender turned me onto was refinancing the existing homes and purchasing new ones in our individual names to give us more purchasing power. Some are in my name only and some are in my husband's. As lending rules stand at the time of this book writing, an individual can finance up to ten properties. As a couple that gives us the ability to own twenty financed homes combined. We like to have our properties financed to take advantage of the power of leverage. More on that later.

USE YOUR HOME EQUITY

With a Home Equity Loan

A home equity loan is a **Second mortgage** on your house with the amount based on the home's equity. You pull out equity in one lump sum and then repay the loan at a fixed rate similar to how you pay your 1st lien mortgage. Equity loans are only permitted on **primary residences** in TX. While the withdrawal and repayment processes differ, the following example will show you how to estimate the amount of equity you can pull out of your home for either a home equity loan or a home equity line of credit.

USE YOUR HOME EQUITY

With a Line of Credit

A home equity line of credit (HELOC) is a line of credit on your home's equity. In Texas you can get a HELOC on your primary residence for the equity you have in your home while still leaving a 20% equity cushion in your home.

For example:

Current market value:	$200,000
Maximum new loan amount* 80%	= 160,000
Existing loan amount	− 100,000
HELOC available	= 60,000

*your mortgage plus the line of credit can't exceed the 80% LTV.

The HELOC is a line of credit, so you only borrow what you need when you need it. I think of it as being like a credit card where you only have to repay the amount you charge.

HELOC interest rates are much lower than credit cards and can be tax deductible.

Check with your CPA on what, if any uses allow for a tax deduction. A HELOC is not allowed on investment property (at least not in Texas).

CHAPTER THREE

Uncle Sam Wants You to Invest

Let's take a few moments to talk about how the government does its best to encourage investment in real estate. There are the obvious tax deductions of writing off mortgage interest and property taxes. When the property is an investment and not your primary residence you get additional benefits such as being able to write off your insurance premium, repairs, maintenance, management fees, etc. Also, the $10k state and local tax write-off maximum doesn't apply to your rentals. You can write it all off. A biggie is the ability to depreciate the structure value of the property on a 27.5 year straight line basis. If I got too accounting technical here you can see a depreciation example off to the side. Or just gloss over this and let your CPA handle it and keep on reading. That reminds me, I can't stress enough that I'm not a CPA nor am I a financial advisor. Consult your professionals to get clarity on these technicalities. What applies to me might not apply to you when it comes to taxes, so the key takeaway here is that there are tax benefits to owning investment property. It's up to you or your CPA to figure out what those are.

More gifts from the government include the ability to leverage the purchase with an amortizing loan. I mean, the principal and

STRAIGHT LINE DEPRECIATION

Accounting rules allow for a structure to be depreciated over 27.5 years. This lets you take the value of the structure and evenly write off depreciation over the 27.5 year term. Visit with your CPA to verify your situation.

For example:

Purchase Price	**$200,000**
Structure Value	**$100,000**
Annual Depreciation	**= 3,636**

~ this is $100,000 / 27.5

Note that the value of the land can not be depreciated, only the structure. Land doesn't lose it's useability but a building does.

interest (P&I) are locked in for thirty years. Think about how effing inexpensive your P&I will be in ten, twenty and thirty years from now if you never refinance. Think about how incredibly inexpensive that will be as compared to the actual market value.

Man alive, then there's leverage! If mortgages can ever be titillating this is why. Here's an example to help you understand if this is a new concept to you. Say you have $40,000 to invest. You could put it in the stock market and get 7% annual returns on average. So, assuming an average year you've made $2,800 or 7% on your money. That's pretty cool. However, if you want super freaking cool then take the same $40k and put it into real estate. This should be enough to cover a 20% down payment on a $200k house (excluding closing costs). The government is a real doll here and lets you put down a fraction of the value of the asset you are acquiring. Aren't they sweet? Using historical average of 5% appreciation of real estate values, your house is worth $210,000 in one year. That's a 25% return on your down payment. See, that's a whole lot cooler than a non-leveraged return even though the non-leveraged average asset appreciation rate is higher. I'll point out that this example is simplified and doesn't account for closing costs, repairs and renovations, vacancy and other costs of acquisition and ownership. On the other hand, it also doesn't account for the benefits of the tax savings it can produce for you. It's a big picture number of looking only at down payment versus market value to show you how powerful leverage can be in generating returns. The net of it is that your gains are ultimately likely to be less than 25% but still much stronger than 7%. Well I've gone and buried the lead here as leverage is the crux of my investment philosophy.

The government lets you leverage your purchase and then they throw the kitchen sink at you in terms of using estimated rental income to offset your debt to income ratio. What the crap-kitty-butt-face did I just say? Let me break it down. There are wicked strict rules to get a mortgage to protect you and our economy on the whole after the 2008 meltdown. To get a mortgage can feel like

LEVERAGE

Using other people's money to increase your rate of return

LEVERAGED PROPERTY
Assumes 5% annual appreciation

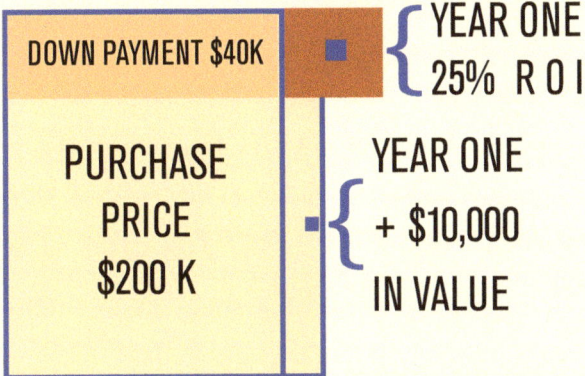

DOWN PAYMENT $40K	{ YEAR ONE 25% R O I
PURCHASE PRICE $200 K	{ YEAR ONE + $10,000 IN VALUE

NON-LEVERAGED (ie STOCK)
Assumes 7% annual appreciation

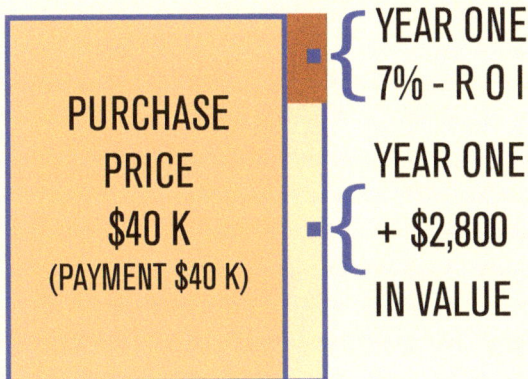

	{ YEAR ONE 7% - R O I
PURCHASE PRICE $40 K (PAYMENT $40 K)	{ YEAR ONE + $2,800 IN VALUE

you are guilty until proven innocent. Or as one particularly awesome client of mine put it—it's like going to the proctologist. But I digress. To get a loan the lender will look at your monthly debt payments on all the loans you have in your name and compare that to how much you make every month. This is what your debt to income ratio (or DTI) is. For conventional financing, your DTI can't exceed 45%. Which means if you have a mortgage already, car payments, student loans, etc., etc., an extra mortgage payment could torpedo your DTI. BUT the government is super cool about this and lets you offset the rental house's mortgage payment by 75% of the anticipated monthly rental income when calculating your DTI. A professional appraiser will establish the anticipated rent income unless you already have a lease in place, then they'll use the amount in the lease agreement. No guesswork is needed on your part.

DEBIT-TO-INCOME RATIO (DTI)

Your DTI is a comparison between your monthly loan payments and your monthly income.

For an investment property, your DTI can't exceed 45%

For example:

If you bring home $10,000 a month, your total loan payments can't exceed $4,500 a month (45% of 10,000 = $4,500)

CHAPTER FOUR

Honey, You Need Money

So, how do you come up with the scratch to get your first rental. I mean, $40k (plus cash for closing and other acquisition costs) might be a lot of coin to have sitting around in your savings. No problem, there are ways to come up with the money by parlaying what you already own. Talk to a good mortgage professional that you trust to find out the options in your home state, but the most typical means of finding the money is by tapping into your home. There are a few ways (at least in Texas) of doing this. There's a home equity loan. This is a 2nd lien on your home that amortizes similar to your first mortgage and may have a balloon payment. There's a home equity line of credit (HELOC) which is a line of credit you can access to borrow against your home's equity. This is like a credit card with a limit that is based on your home's equity that has a much better interest rate than a real credit card. Then there's the cash-out refinance, which is getting a new primary mortgage on your home and pocketing the equity between the new mortgage and the previous mortgage that gets paid off when you complete the refinance. Any way you slice it, these funds are not taxed. Be aware that there are typically closing costs to refinancing and your new monthly mortgage payment is likely to be higher than the previous one. Also, depending on the terms, refinancing can extend the length of time to reach the moment you have the home paid off. Talk to a trusted mortgage lender to understand the best loan type for you and how the terms bear out in your situation. (See pages 6 and 12-13)

Well, hell, what if you don't own your own house yet? Start by getting your own home and work your way into this game. Remember this is a get rich slow plan. You might have an advantage over those of us who already own a home because you can go about your first purchase more intentionally to position yourself for success from the beginning. Think living closer to bars and clubs versus a manicured suburban utopia. This house can either make a great rental one day or will make you enough money to buy rentals and a better house to move into. One exception to the plan of attack of buying your primary residence first are my peeps in Silicon Valley that don't own their home but make mad cash at their fancy tech jobs.

CHAPTER FIVE

Pick a Winner

What and where would you buy? And for how much? This is open to interpretation and it's hard to get this wrong if you follow the basic fundamentals I'm going to outline for you. It allows for a lot of flexibility to match your preferences.

First and foremost, finding a good deal that is on the market through properties listed for sale by a real estate broker is where the easiest pickings can be found. Since this is a long-term buy and hold approach, scrounging around for the elusive off market deal with wackadoodle financing sources isn't necessary. Let those flipper guys do their thing and you focus on having a life while you get rich slow. Don't go and make a simple thing unnecessarily hard.

I identify a good investment in Austin by backing into it. In the order of operations of acquiring a property, the last step is getting a tenant placed in the property. Let's start with the end in mind. We want getting a tenant to be easy and it is made easy by appealing to the biggest portion of the tenant population that is likely to stay in the property for multiple years. In Austin today the largest portion of the tenant population is renting in the $1400-$1900 range. This sweet spot price range changes, but the idea behind it doesn't. Anyone who can afford more than $1900 (or whatever the top number is in your market currently) is likely to buy their own home, which leaves you with higher turnover. Also, there are fewer people in the $1900+ price range than there are in the $1400-$1900 range.

Why do we want to avoid turnover? Vacancies are one of the biggest expenses in owning a rental since nobody is helping you pay the mortgage during a vacancy. Then there are the leasing fees if you are paying a property manager to find the tenant for you. Tenants who are renting in the sweet spot range are more likely to be forever renters with no designs on ever owning their own home. They won't stay in your house forever, but they are more likely to stay for more than one year.

Another interesting aspect to reinforce the power of staying inside of the sweet spot range is that, at least in Austin, rents and property value don't move in lockstep. What does that mean? Well, here in Austin a typical $200k house will rent for around $1500/mo. A typical $600k house will rent for $3000/mo. If they moved in tandem, then the $600k house would rent for $4500/mo.; this means that once you go beyond the top of the sweet spot of rent prices you begin to subsidize the lifestyle of your tenant.

Continuing to back into how to locate a property, let's take the sweet spot range of rent and see how that matches up to your mortgage payment—principal, interest, taxes, insurance (PITI) —assuming a 20% down payment. That gives you the price range to be looking in where you'll be more or less cash flow neutral (of course cash flow positive is better and slightly negative can be feasible depending on the deal). That means we want a house where the price and rent jibe.

MONTHLY GROSS RENT MULTIPLIER

MGRM = purchase price ÷ monthly rent

- Your MGRM is calculated by taking your purchase price and dividing by your monthly rent.
- A top end MGRM is 150, less is better.
- Another way of looking at it is to multiply your estimated monthly rent by 150 to get an ideal top end purchase price:

Purchase price = 150 x monthly rent

A shortcut to getting to the ideal property purchase price range is to use a formula called the Monthly Gross Rent Multiplier (MGRM). This is the property price divided by monthly rent. If this number is 150 or less, you are within the sweet spot. Why 150 or less? The best way I can explain it is it is just how it factors out. Monthly rent times 150 or less will get you to the price range you want to be in where your cash flow works and you're not subsidizing your tenant's lifestyle.

Areas of town where rent and sales price work in harmony is the next step of keying in on what to buy. This is a VERY important step even though it didn't go first in my analysis. Location, location, location is a popular saying because it's totally true. In Austin the most valuable land is located downtown. It's so expensive that the houses are stacked vertically into high rises. As you move out from the city center, the land remains valuable and decreases somewhat the farther you move out. Think of it as the layers of an onion. Every time we have an economic boom and the population grows, what is considered close-in and valuable expands out to the next layer toward the outside of the onion. You want to buy right on the cusp of the next outer layer to get "discovered" as the next great place to live. While downtown is our core of land value, there are smaller onions all over the metro area that generate their own centers of land value. These smaller-value-generating points of interest include employers, improved infrastructure (toll roads, highway expansions), shopping, entertainment, colleges, hospitals, parks, anything that draws people to stay close to the area, and spend time and money within a small radius.

It's also important to make sure the area you identify is landlocked by other development as opposed to being adjacent to vacant land. Living near new residential construction will depress your appreciation potential. Being in an area that is already built-out puts you way ahead on the road to appreciation. Why? Because developed land near points of interest is more valuable than swaths of vacant land. It's the dirt you really care about over the long run. Think about this: a new house on the outskirts of town has very little land value and the structure is what generates the price. I've seen price lists by developers in the exurbs with the lot value listed at $2,000. They obviously don't think very highly of the location of that lot! On top of that, structures depreciate quickly. In ten years this new house will have outdated finishes and the walls, roof, and all its components will be less valuable. That's why the IRS lets investors depreciate the structure. When you buy a house that is in a built-

RICH SLOW IS MY HOMEBOY

up area, the house is probably already depreciated and the land is the primary source of the value. That's why people move far out of town to "get more for their money" in the form of a great big new house for the same price as an older, smaller house closer to town. Because of this principle, most of the houses I buy or encourage my clients to buy are older. That might not be the same situation in your city, this is just how Austin is laid out. The houses I'm buying now were once in the outskirts but now they are in the thick of it all. Get good help to figure out what works where you live or where you want to invest. If you're in Austin, I'm that good help!

Location and price are a moving target, but the underlying fundamentals don't change. For example, when I first started investing I was purchasing homes within the city limits. The sweet spot range of rents and pricing have changed and I've been effectively chased out of Austin and am now focused on the northern suburbs. Why north and not south? All of Austin is legit for investing depending on your goals and approach, but I find north to have more potential. There is a development called The Domain that is effectively a second downtown filled with tech companies and it is located in North Austin. If Disney created a squeaky clean bougie downtown it would look a lot like The Domain. An interesting and important fact is that it is located north because it's at the geographic center of the Austin area population. South Austin is real swell but it doesn't have an equivalent to The Domain. Investing on the north side is a personal preference that is influenced heavily by the fundamentals I practice. People invest all over town for their own reasons. Have a North Star of fundamentals you want to abide by when you invest. The Dude abides and I want you to also.

Should you buy a fixer-upper? Maybe. This approach has leeway for flexibility and there's no rigid answer to this. I have clients who prefer to buy at a discount and then add value. I have other clients who prefer to buy a place that's already looking good so they can get it rented out faster. Also, when you buy a house that's already in good shape you are putting 20% down on the sales price and money is cheap these days with low interest rates, so financing a higher sales price can be compelling as compared to getting a cheaper place and putting money into it. When you fix it up yourself you are financing 100% of the improvements in most cases. So even if you are paying a premium for a house that someone already worked on, you might come out ahead in terms of cash outflow thus making the next acquisition possible sooner. Keep all options on the table until you know what works for you.

What kind of condition should a rental be in? My method is to make sure all the systems are operating and in good shape before a tenant moves in to minimize inconvenience for both parties. I also like to have my units just cute enough where it will rent faster and for a bit more money than a dumpier but mostly equivalent property. I avoid carpet as much as possible for obvious reasons. Fresh clean paint, fairly nice, big-box quality fans and fixtures, wood-look flooring (tile or vinyl plank), granite and subway tile are good finishes to aim for. Tenants choose a house with a consumption mindset rather than an investment mindset. That's a fancy way of saying they'll pay more to live in a cuter house. But don't go too crazy making it nice. Evaluate the return on your investment so you don't over-improve the property.

What else do I like in a property? Something with an obvious exit

RICH SLOW IS MY HOMEBOY

strategy. I focus on one-story, single family homes. These are basic 3 bed, 2 bath starter homes that I liken to little green Monopoly houses. Because of the other fundamentals of age, location and price, they all tend to fall in the 1200-to-1600-square-foot range. I don't look for houses that size, that's just how big they are in this market. It's like the Model T coming in only black. It is what it is and it's the norm so nobody gets their panties in a wad about it. I've learned to preemptively tell my clients that all these houses have small bedrooms and closets because so many got their panties in a wad about it that I ended up getting my panties in a wad about them having their panties in a wad. I mean, how big can a bedroom be in a 3-bedroom 1200-square-foot house? Geez! The people who live and rent in these homes are chill with the dimensions. Let's all relax now.

Why not a two-story? Two-story homes can turn off people with small kids or mobility issues. Also, I say this jokingly, but something about two stories makes tenants really want to overflow the tub or toilet so it wrecks the ceiling on the first floor. Then if you need to paint siding on the second level, painters rightfully want to be paid for the scaffolding and all that extra BS they have to contend with.

Why not multifamily? Well, in my city multifamily is hard to come by and they are typically situated in pockets with other duplex, triplex, and fourplexes. These areas tend to be rundown. Your city may be completely different; I can't speak to specifics of your city if you're outside of Austin. Around here one negligent landlord can bring down the whole area. When you go to sell you are stuck selling to another investor who is likely to beat you up as much as possible on price. Also, being in a pocket of many multifamily properties makes it hard for you to fix up your place and get a nice premium if all the neighbors look like crap.

A one-story, single-family home can appeal to many walks of life. Unlike multifamily, it has stronger potential to fix it up enough to sell for a premium. I don't recommend selling too soon since we are talking about a buy and long-term hold philosophy, but something with a good exit strategy is also something that has strong appreciation potential. Remember, we are talking about getting rich slow and have discussed my thinking on flipping.

These houses and neighborhoods might not be as cute and manicured as yours. That's the whole point. They have room for improvement and these neighborhoods are emerging or having a resurgence of appeal based on what is going on around them that increases the value of the whole area. Once upon a time these neighborhoods might have been out in the hinterlands and fell into a bit of disrepair over time. Now that the city has caught up and grown up around them, they are about to be cool again.

CHAPTER SIX

Climbing the Retirement Ladder

What's the end game here to retire in style? I have an answer for me and my family that has me very, very excited. It might not be the right answer for you, but it will give you some food for thought. Remember the good old cash-out refinance? It revolves around that. This sweetheart of a financing vehicle not only let me double my portfolio size, it is anticipated that it will fund our retirement assuming today's lending rules and appreciation and inflation averages hold. Nobody can be sure what the future really holds, but my plan is well-grounded in verifiable assumptions.

After doing my round of cash-out refinances, I began telling my clients about it and helping them see the possibility it presented for growing their portfolio. My advice is to aggressively grow your portfolio now and use the power of the cash-out refinance to propel this growth. Depending on appreciation, every four to seven years you can cash-out refinance your properties and reinvest the proceeds to double the size of your portfolio. Rinse and repeat as often as possible. Then at a point when retirement is ten-to-fifteen years away, stop refinancing the houses and let appreciation and amortization grow your equity so you can begin to harvest.

REFI RETIREMENT LADDER

First climb up the ladder
(1st Refi on each property)

Age	Year[1]	Property Number	Market Value	Proceeds Withdrawn[2]
60	1	1	$650,000	$248,000
61	2	2	$688,000	$260,000
62	3	3	$662,000	$248,000
63	4	4	$695,000	$252,000
64	5	5	$597,000	$216,000
65	6	6	$627,000	$222,000
66	7	7	$658,000	$226,000
67	8	8	$691,000	$236,000
68	9	9	$677,000	$224,000
69	10	10	$693,000	$224,000

[1]Year count of retirement
[2]Proceeds withdrawn are net of the existing mortgage balance before the cash-out refinance and have been adjusted for inflation.

Average annual assumptions:

- Inflation 3%   • Appreciation - 5%

Cash out refinance new loans are based on 75% loan-to-value ratio.

RICH SLOW IS MY HOMEBOY

REFI RETIREMENT LADDER

Second climb up the ladder
(2nd Refi on each property)
Supplemental retirement funds may be required

Age	Year[1]	Property Number	Market Value	Proceeds Withdrawn[2]
70	11	1	$1,059,000	$185,000
71	12	2	$1,120,000	$190,000
72	13	3	$1,078,000	$178,000
73	14	4	$1,132,000	$181,000
74	15	5	$ 972,000	$151,000
75	16	6	$1,021,000	$154,000
76	17	7	$1,072,000	$157,000
77	18	8	$1,126,000	$160,000
78	19	9	$1,103,000	$152,000
79	20	10	$1,129,000	$151,000

[1] Year count of retirement
[2] Proceeds withdrawn are net of the existing mortgage balance before the cash-out refinance and have been adjusted for inflation.

Average annual assumptions:

- Inflation 3%   - Appreciation - 5%

Cash out refinance new loans are based on 75% loan-to-value ratio.

I call my personal plan a laddering approach because it entails cash-out refinancing one property every twelve months and living off the equity tax-free. This should provide enough income to get us at or above the $200k/year income range (adjusted for anticipated inflation) without paying taxes on it and without tapping into our 401(k)s initially. Let me illustrate.

The year I turn sixty we will do a cash-out refinance on one of the rental houses and be able to pull out enough equity to live a good life without suffering financially. In the next twelve months we will cash-out refinance the second house. This pattern will continue until we have cashed all ten of them out through refinancing. That will be twenty-five years from now (fifteen years until age sixty plus ten years to complete the first cycle of cashing out each home).

Since we did cash-out refinances, we still own all ten rentals. During the eleventh year of retirement (twenty-six years from now) we will start over, doing the cash-out refinances beginning with the first house we cash-out refinance when I turn sixty. At this point my projections indicate we will need to begin tapping into our 401(k) accounts to supplement our income but will keep us safe from taking out so much that we reduce the principle. That means throughout years eleven to twenty we go through the ladder again of cash-out refinancing a property every year or so. The graphic on the previous pages illustrates what this laddering approach looks like. The numbers I share in the graphic are an adaptation of what my personal numbers might be assuming my projections hold over the years. While these aren't my precise numbers (my mother taught me to leave something to the imagination), they give you a sense of what can be possible in a similar situation.

Year twenty-one of the ladder? This is really far out since it's thirty-six years from today. But assuming we are still in this dimension of incarnation, at that point we might consider selling one a year as my models indicate that may be a strong move to make to have funds to get us to 100 years old and still leave a sizable estate to our kids. Or maybe we'll refinance some more. It's a high-quality problem to have to figure this out.

I don't plan to stop at ten investment homes. Just recently we had only nine of them until I ran a spreadsheet model to see the effect of adding another house to our portfolio. Let's just say that I had property number ten under contract in a week after running my model. Time and compounding are your friends if you take the time to get to know them and use their superpowers. Adding another house wasn't just a plus-one. It affects all of the houses. Every year that I can extend the ladder, it gives each house that much longer to appreciate and for the mortgage to amortize. This also reduces our need to draw on our 401(k)s, which has it's own compounding effect. If I live to age 100, the $215k house I just bought today will make our estate $2.6M more valuable in today's dollars.

Following this logic, if I buy another house next year it will go to the end of the ladder and it will have twenty-five years to appreciate and amortize before we cash-out refinance it and the other ten will enjoy the extended runway of compounding in value. If I buy property number twelve the year after next it will too be twenty-five years before we are ready to extract equity. This pattern continues. Every addition has twenty-five years to season while giving the entire portfolio an additional year to compound. As mentioned previously, these additional properties also benefit the size and longevity of our 401(k)s.

I should mention that if our burn rate (burn rate is a swaggery MBA term that means pace of spending) allows it, we can postpone our cash-out refinances to happen less frequently than every twelve months. That, too, will have a huge compounding impact on our portfolio value and longevity of wealth.

Oh yeah, I haven't addressed rent here because it's not the motivator. My model assumes rent is on par with expenses, although I expect in reality it will exceed expenses and we will have a decent amount of positive cash flow during the earlier years of our first ladder climb. To be as thorough as possible with our real estate options in retirement, I ran a scenario where we pay off the houses and live off the rent and it was quickly very apparent that is significantly less financially efficient. This is because we have such strong appreciation in this market that it beats the pulp out of rental income. Also, in Austin property taxes are crazy high. We don't have state income taxes so they tax the living crap out of our homes, which makes projecting carrying costs that far into the future pretty tricky.

Another item I haven't gone into in depth about is how we are going to be able to qualify for the cash-out refinances if we are no longer earning income. This is a highly valid consideration and it will likely rely on the cash flow we are making from rent and pulling money from our 401(k) to show income but then putting that money right back into investment accounts. Lending rules of the future will dictate what's possible. But looking at today's rules, my plan is set to work.

CHAPTER SEVEN

Yeah But

Time for the buts. I've given you the rainbows and unicorns of investing and now it's time to talk about the shadow side. There are risks and inconveniences involved in real estate investing. To me, they just aren't nearly matched up to get close to defeating the benefits of doing it. Really, so much of the hard part of having rentals can be alleviated by hiring a good property manager. In my market you can get good management for $99 a month. For the value they provide, that is a stone-cold no-brainer. I do have plenty of clients that happily self-manage. I just don't have the stomach, time or patience for it.

I have this same investment conversation with lots of folks. I've found that about 30% actually follow through with purchasing a home. Of this 30% about half come back for more once they get settled with the idea of owning investment property. It seems to take most people about one year to realize it's not fatal and they'd like to do it again. The other half are contented with their one property and glad they made the purchase. The 70% that don't buy anything is because they aren't willing to put forth the time and effort to learn the market and identify a good home to purchase, or with some people it's the idea of owning another home that just freaks them out too much. That's cool by me. I acknowledge them for taking the time to learn about investing using the philosophy I teach.

It's a legit concern that the market might take a turn for the worse and your property will lose value for a period of time. We all have to deal with it; it's reality's operations that the market is cyclical. The good news is that this is a buy-and-hold strategy, so downturns don't matter so much because it's always a good time to buy, it's just not always a good time to sell. It is my practice and my advice to take the news reports about housing with a grain of salt. Have you noticed that different reporters and news outlets print conflicting opinions? I think they want us to be confused so we keep coming back for more in a misguided attempt to get real clarity. Stay focused on the fundamentals of reality; the market will come back and likely better than before. When there's a downturn just hold onto your butts and wait. Better yet, when there is a downturn quit playing with your butt and get out there and buy if you can. What sucks for me is that I sell real estate for a living, so having the funds and cojones for investing during a downturn is not always possible. But that might be a golden opportunity for you if you're in a different industry.

I just mentioned that it's always a good time to buy. Many clients show up wondering if there is an optimal time of year to buy. My answer is always the same—absolutely, the best time to buy is the exact time of year when you are ready to make the effort to buy. Sure, there is a high season where it's easier to fill a vacancy, but lease terms can be adjusted to get you on a summer lease expiration schedule. Last year I had three vacancies come up in November and we filled them pretty quickly, thanks in part to a small discount on

RICH SLOW IS MY HOMEBOY

rent to get people in the door. Two of the three families agreed to an eighteen-month lease so now we are going to be in the best season for finding a new tenant when those two leases come due should these current people decide to split.

Don't forget that humans live in these houses. One house I own accepted tenants who signed a twelve-month lease during the springtime. I thought I was in good shape until the following September when the female tenant let my manager know that her boyfriend / meal ticket left her and she couldn't make rent and was moving out. I saw it as half full and I was grateful she got out quickly. I knew we wouldn't see the reletting fee that she technically owed, so we just cut ties and got busy trying to find a tenant in October. My thinking is that you can't get into a bad mood about these situations because it does you no good. There is absolutely a level of adulthood that comes with being a landlord. Stay focused on the big picture and know that stuff like this comes with the territory and none of us is special enough to not have it happen. Steady on, old chap.

Who came up with the well-known scary story about the call in the middle of the night to the landlord because the toilet is clogged? As far as my experience goes that's an urban legend. Think about this. If you were a tenant and managed to clog a toilet after midnight wouldn't you be a bit embarrassed about what it took to get yourself into that position? Wouldn't you go back to bed and plunger it in the morning to maintain your dignity? I'm not saying that things don't break and go wrong in all sorts of interesting ways. It's just that it might not be as severe as you are bracing yourself for. I rest easier because my property manager deals with these issues.

Regardless of whether you have a property manager, any property will cost you money over the years to keep it in good shape. Just like any house, things need updating, repairs and replacement. Some repairs are inexpensive and others, like a new roof, are less frequent but more costly.

You don't like pets? Same here but my landlord alter ego loves them! Most tenants want to rent a house instead of an apartment because they have pets. I recommend being pet friendly, getting a pet deposit, and having pet resistant finishes in the house (i.e., no carpet).

What about vacation rentals? I'll be brief because it's not my thang. It depends on location, economics and your local political climate about their legality. I'll take this opportunity to hawk my brother's book, *Master of Vacation Rentals* by Jeff Pierce. He's got that topic covered for you in a really good read.

What about flipping? Flipping works for some but not most people. The ones with the best chances of success are contractors or have other means of getting labor and materials at below-market rates. To me it's just too speculative. The financing on those sorts of deals can be tricky and scary if you're green at it. Again, I'm not a CPA, but my guess is you pay taxes on your gains when you sell a flip. When you hold a property and refinance it to access your equity through a cash-out refinance, it's not taxable. Also, if you find a really good property, what's the rush to sell it? If it's so great it will continue to appreciate well and, if you leveraged it, your returns will be oh-so-sweet and lovely.

When it comes to cash-out refinances, consult a trusted mortgage advisor so you can understand what it takes to pull equity out of your property. There are closing costs involved and your new monthly payment is likely to be higher than your previous one. Besides your creditworthiness to get a loan, there are maximums you can pull out of the property. This means that you have to qualify for the loan and your property also has to qualify.

CHAPTER EIGHT

Nerdy Stuff You Might be Wondering About

Insurance

What's the best way to insure the property? Talk to your lender and insurance agent. Most lenders require a fire policy that covers the property but not the contents. Your tenants should get their own renters' policy to cover their stuff. A wise line of defense as the landlord is to have an umbrella policy to cover all your assets and vehicles. These are fairly inexpensive and you can get coverage in the millions of dollars. I'm not an insurance agent, so have your own conversation to see what's best for you and your situation.

Legal Entities

Can I and should I put my property into a legal entity? I have to step very carefully here because I am not an attorney and I hold a real estate license in Texas. My answer is to talk to your attorney. CYA accomplished.

Property Management

Should I hire a property manager or DIY this B? It depends. I have plenty of clients who go in either direction. My advice is to, at a minimum, have a competent property manager help you find the tenant. This will cost you up to one month's rent, but it will save you many headaches of coordinating property tours. It might shock you that tenants might not show up for a scheduled appointment to see your house. A property manager can do the marketing, determine pricing, stay within fair housing guidelines, and perform the litany of background checks: credit, criminal history, employment verification, rental history. They also will write up the paperwork for you. To me this is well worth the cost.

Some folks try out managing on their own with the knowledge they can turn the property over to a manager in a moment's notice if they feel they are in over their heads. Others jump right in because they ain't got time to handle the following: renewing leases on time, raising rent adequately each year, enforcing rules, coordinating repairs, bookkeeping, collecting rent, following fair housing, dealing with evictions.

Evictions?! Oh crap, do those happen? Yes, they do but it's fairly rare. Having a manager do the vetting to approve a tenant can help minimize your exposure. I have been through one eviction a long time ago when I was managing my properties on my own. It was not fun, but we were able to run the ne'er do wells (they had used a stolen identity while applying for the house and were living off of stolen credit cards) off as quickly as the law allowed. I was very motivated to get those wonderful human beings out of my house since I had a baby on the way. When the big day came to lawfully get their asses out of my house, I met the constable at the curb and we went to the front door together. I was 8.5 months pregnant and he had a pistol with a mother of pearl inlay on his hip. We were looking pretty awesome together. Fortunately, they had already vacated the property but left all sorts of filth behind. These days I would have a property manager handle the whole thing. Why didn't I have a manger do it for me then? Because I didn't know I could. I didn't have this book to help show me the way.

CHAPTER NINE

Final Words

At the end of the day put together your team of domain-specific specialists to get you going. You don't have to do this on your own or be an expert at all aspects. I recommend asking people you hold in high regard for referrals to make sure you're getting connected with powerful, proven professionals. Some of the specialties you'll want to engage are: Realtor, lender, CPA, insurance agent, attorney, property manager, and contractors. Leverage your network to create more and more powerful networks. I have many colleagues and industry-related contacts to thank for honing this investment philosophy with me. I'm fortunate to have surrounded myself with a powerful network. In no way did I come up with all this on my own. I just like to write and am highly passionate about this topic so decided to make a book about it. Thank you for reading it! Live long and prosper.

www.ingramcontent.com/pod-product-compliance
Lightning Source LLC
Chambersburg PA
CBHW040910210326
41597CB00029B/5041